IMAN VELLANI

Making a Difference as a Young Superhero

I0794151

By Katie Kawa

KidHaven
PUBLISHING

People Who Make a Difference

Published in 2025 by
KidHaven Publishing, an Imprint of Greenhaven Publishing, LLC
2544 Clinton St.
Buffalo, NY 14224

Designer: Deanna Lepovich
Editor: Katie Kawa

Photo credits: Cover lev radin/Shutterstock.com; p. 5, 17 Matt Crossick/Alamy Stock Photo; p. 7 Image Press Agency/Alamy Stock Photo; p. 9 (main) dpa picture alliance/Alamy Stock Photo; p. 9 (inset) Denis Makarenko/Shutterstock.com; p. 11, 20 Abaca Press/Alamy Stock Photo; p. 13 MediaPunch Inc/Alamy Stock Photo; p. 15 Tea Talk/Shutterstock.com; p. 19 BFA/Alamy Stock Photo; p. 21 T.Sumaetho/Shutterstock.com.

Library of Congress Cataloging-in-Publication Data

Names: Kawa, Katie, author.
Title: Iman Vellani : making a difference as a young superhero / Katie Kawa.
Description: Buffalo, New York : KidHaven Publishing, [2025] | Series: People who make a difference | Includes index.
Identifiers: LCCN 2024009019 | ISBN 9781534548046 (library binding) | ISBN 9781534548039 (paperback) | ISBN 9781534548053 (ebook)
Subjects: LCSH: Vellani, Iman–Juvenile literature. | Motion picture actors and actresses–Canada–Biography–Juvenile literature. | Marvel, Ms. (Fictitious character)–Juvenile literature. | LCGFT: Biographies.
Classification: LCC PN2308.V45 K39 2025 | DDC 791.4302/8092 [B]–dc23/eng/20240319
LC record available at https://lccn.loc.gov/2024009019

Printed in the United States of America

CPSIA compliance information: Batch #CSKH25: For further information contact Greenhaven Publishing LLC at 1-844-317-7404.

Please visit our website, www.greenhavenpublishing.com. For a free color catalog of all our high-quality books, call toll free 1-844-317-7404 or fax 1-844-317-7405.

Find us on

CONTENTS

FROM SUPERFAN TO SUPERHERO

Millions of people around the world love to read **comic books** and watch superhero movies. Iman Vellani is one of them! She grew up loving the **Marvel Cinematic Universe** (MCU) movies and comic books that told the story of the young superhero Ms. Marvel (who is also known as Kamala Khan).

Today, Iman is still a fan. However, she's not just reading and watching superhero stories—she's helping create them! Iman went from reading about Ms. Marvel to playing her in the MCU. Her story has **inspired** many people—just like Ms. Marvel's story inspires her.

In Her Words

"Kamala getting her powers and me getting this part really went hand-in-hand. We went on this journey of self-discovery together."

— Interview with *Variety* magazine from June 2022

The actress Iman Vellani and the character Ms. Marvel are both Muslims with roots in Pakistan. By bringing Ms. Marvel to life, Iman has helped create positive **representation** for Muslims in the world of superhero movies and TV shows.

ROOTS IN PAKISTAN

Iman Vellani was born in 2002 in Karachi, which is a city in the South Asian nation of Pakistan. Her first name means "faith" in the Arabic language. This is the language used in the Quran, which is the holy book for Muslims—people who follow the religion, or belief system, of Islam.

Iman was raised in the Islamic faith. Her family worked to stay connected to their roots even after moving from Pakistan to Canada when Iman was 1 year old. Iman grew up in a part of Canada called Ontario, close to the major city of Toronto.

In Her Words

"Names are so important and, I can say this for myself, as soon as I [came] to terms with how cool my name is and how rare [special] it is for people to have a name like mine, it's a big step to take in self-acceptance."

— Interview with *Variety* magazine from June 2022

Iman has said that playing Kamala Khan—a young woman learning to understand herself and where she comes from—has helped her feel more connected to her Pakistani Muslim **culture**.

THE NEXT WAVE

Iman found ways to make a difference even before she became Ms. Marvel. While she was still a student at Unionville High School, she was chosen to be part of the TIFF Next Wave Committee for 2019 to 2020. This was a group of young people that worked as part of TIFF—the Toronto International Film Festival.

The job of the committee was to call attention to movies playing at a festival, or event, that were important for young people to see. Iman was a good choice for this group because she loved movies and wanted to share new points of view.

In Her Words

"We want stories from different **genders** and different countries and different people … I think that's really important because then people are going to understand each other. Even if they can't **relate** to it, you learn from it."

— Interview with CBC News from September 2019

Iman isn't the only famous actor who went to Unionville High School. Hayden Christensen, who's played Anakin Skywalker in the *Star Wars* movies and TV shows, also went to that school!

THE LIFE OF A FANGIRL

When Iman was in high school, she was like most teenage girls her age. She had interests she cared a lot about. One of those interests was the world of superheroes.

Iman loved the movies of the MCU, and she was a huge fan of Iron Man (also known as Tony Stark). She also loved reading comic books about Ms. Marvel. She even made her own Ms. Marvel costume! Iman saw a lot of herself in that character, who was Marvel's first Muslim superhero. Ms. Marvel wasn't part of the MCU yet, but that was about to change.

In Her Words

"I hope [audiences] find comfort in Kamala because I definitely did when I read those comics the first time."

— Interview with *Variety* magazine from June 2022

Before Iman was posing with MCU stars like Simu Liu (shown here) on the red carpet, she was just a fan. She used to share her ideas about Marvel movies and comics online and wrote her own stories about Ms. Marvel in her journal.

GETTING THE PART

It was time to bring Ms. Marvel into the MCU, but finding the right actress to play her took time. Iman's aunt heard about auditions, or tryouts, for the *Ms. Marvel* TV show, and she told Iman about it. Iman almost didn't try out, but she knew her younger self would have done anything to play this part. So, she made a tape of herself trying out and waited to hear if she got the part.

Iman got the part, and in 2020, it was announced that she would be playing Ms. Marvel. Iman was about to live her dream!

In Her Words

"It's so wonderful: I got to go on this journey with Kamala of reconnecting with my roots and finding the value in how important it is to be in touch with that side of yourself. Otherwise, it's just going to get lost, and you're never going to find out who you are."

— Interview with *Entertainment Weekly* magazine from June 2022

Iman studied acting in high school, but playing Ms. Marvel was her first real acting job! She got the part right at the end of her last year of high school.

FEELING SEEN

Iman's first job in the MCU was *Ms. Marvel*—a TV show about how Kamala Khan got her powers and learned to balance being a superhero with her life at school and with her family. The show came out on Disney+ in June 2022.

People loved the show, but one group found it especially meaningful. Muslim fans of the MCU loved seeing a show that represented them in a positive way. Many of the people who worked on the show, including Iman, were Muslims. They wanted to fight harmful **stereotypes** about their religion by showing a loving, joyful Muslim family and community.

In Her Words

"Film and TV shape how we see people in this world, and there are two billion Muslims in the world—that's one in four people … When you represent them in a way that reflects [shows] the way they actually live, it can open people's eyes."

— Interview with *Harper's Bazaar* magazine from June 2022

Ms. Marvel shows many aspects, or parts, of life for Muslims with Pakistani roots. For example, it shows how Muslims get ready to attend services at a mosque, which is their meeting place for prayer. It also shows what a Pakistani wedding is like. It was important for Iman and the rest of the team behind *Ms. Marvel* to represent this community in an accurate, or truthful, way.

BECOMING A WRITER

Iman's belief in the power of positive representation has earned her many fans. Many of her fans also love how much she knows about and cares about the MCU and the comics that inspired it.

Iman's knowledge of comic books, especially ones about Ms. Marvel, helped her get another job. Marvel Comics asked her to help write a **limited series** of Ms. Marvel comics called *Ms. Marvel: The New Mutant*. The first of these comics came out in August 2023. Iman worked on these comics with Sabir Pirzada, who also wrote an episode of *Ms. Marvel*.

In Her Words

"It's … so **surreal** the fact [that] the words that I'm writing I wrote in my childhood bedroom and now people are going to read it in their homes."

— Interview with Marvel.com from August 2023

Iman has said that some of the things she wrote in *Ms. Marvel: The New Mutant* were parts of stories she wrote in her journal when she was younger.

TEAMING UP

In November 2023, Iman played Kamala Khan in *The Marvels*. This movie also starred Brie Larson as Captain Marvel (also known as Carol Danvers) and Teyonah Parris as Monica Rambeau. It was directed by Nia DaCosta, who became the first Black woman to direct a major superhero movie.

It's still rare for superhero movies to **focus** on female characters, but this movie tells the story of three female superheroes. That's why *The Marvels* inspired female fans. When people see characters who look like them doing great things, it helps them believe they're great too.

In Her Words

"The work's not done just because you have one superhero. It's not even close, you know?"

— Interview with *Cosmopolitan* magazine from November 2023

The Life of Iman Vellani

2002
Iman Vellani is born in Karachi, Pakistan.

2003
Iman and her family move to Ontario, Canada.

2019
Iman is chosen to be part of the TIFF Next Wave Committee.

2020
Iman is chosen to play Ms. Marvel in the MCU.

2022
Ms. Marvel airs on Disney+.

2023
The first *Ms. Marvel: The New Mutant* comic book comes out in August, and *The Marvels* comes out in November.

Iman Vellani has just started to make a difference in the movie and TV business, and her future looks bright!

REPRESENTATION MATTERS

Iman has said many times that she wants to tell more of Kamala's story, and it seems like she'll have a chance to do just that in the future. She's very popular with Marvel fans, and Ms. Marvel has become an important character in the MCU.

Iman has made a difference by helping young women, Muslims, and people of Pakistani **descent** feel seen on the big screen and on TV. She's inspiring them to believe in themselves the same way the character of Ms. Marvel inspired her. Representation matters, and Iman Vellani's story shows us that in a powerful way.

In Her Words

"*Ms. Marvel* isn't the end, it's just the start. I really hope that it inspires more Muslim and South Asian creatives to tell their stories."

— Interview with *Harper's Bazaar* magazine from June 2022

Be Like Iman Vellani!

Learn more about different cultures and religions.

Learn about your background and culture, and share it with your friends.

Watch movies and TV shows that are examples of positive representation for different groups.

Keep a journal to practice sharing who you are and what matters to you through writing. Maybe you can write a story starring a character you love!

Be respectful of people from different cultures and who practice different religions.

Be yourself, and be proud to be a fan of the things you love. Support other fans, too, and treat them with respect.

Talk to your family members and friends about the movies and TV shows you're watching and if they're examples of positive representation or negative stereotypes.

Tell your friends to share their stories through writing, music, or another kind of art, and support them when they do.

Iman Vellani plays a superhero in movies and on TV, but she doesn't need superpowers to make a difference. These are just some ways you can follow her lead and use your powers for good!

GLOSSARY

comic book: A kind of magazine or book that contains cartoons grouped together that tell a story.

culture: The beliefs and ways of life of a certain group of people.

descent: The background of a person in terms of their family or nationality.

focus: To direct attention or effort at something.

gender: The state of being male, female, some combination of the two, or neither male nor female.

inspire: To move someone to do something great.

limited series: A group of comic books telling a connected story that has a set number of issues that is known before the first issue comes out.

Marvel Cinematic Universe: The group of Marvel movies and TV shows that share many of the same characters and began with *Iron Man* in 2008.

relate: To connect, understand, or respond, especially in a favorable way.

representation: The act of showing a group in a movie, TV show, or another kind of media.

stereotype: An idea that's formed about all people of a certain group that's often untrue or only partly true.

surreal: Like a dream.

FOR MORE INFORMATION

WEBSITES

Iman Vellani: Creator Spotlight

www.marvel.com/comics/discover/2410/iman-vellani

Check out this part of the Marvel website to learn about Iman Vellani's favorite comic books.

IMDb: Iman Vellani

www.imdb.com/name/nm11940123/

Iman Vellani's page on the Internet Movie Database presents facts about her life and the movies and TV shows she's made.

BOOKS

Horning, Nicole. *A Modern Nerd's Guide to Comic Books.* Buffalo, NY: Gareth Stevens Publishing, 2020.

Green, Meghan. *What's Representation?* Buffalo, NY: KidHaven Publishing, 2024.

London, Martha. *Brie Larson.* Lake Elmo, MN: Focus Readers, 2021.

Publisher's note to educators and parents: Our editors have carefully reviewed these websites to ensure that they are suitable for students. Many websites change frequently, however, and we cannot guarantee that a site's future contents will continue to meet our high standards of quality and educational value. Be advised that students should be closely supervised whenever they access the internet.

INDEX